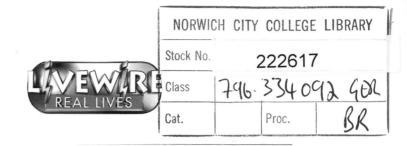

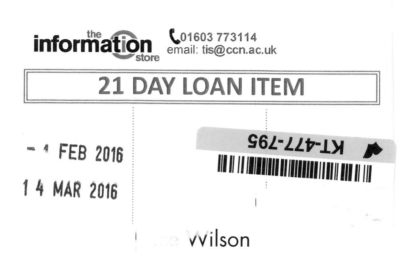

Wilson

Published in association with The Basic Skills Agency

Hodder Murray

A MEMBER OF THE HODDER HEADLINE GROUP

Acknowledgements
Photo credits
p.iv © Matthew Ashton/EMPICS; p.8 © Ross Kinnaird/Getty Images; p.11 © MARTYN
HARRISON/AFP/Getty Images; p.15 © Adam Davy/EMPICS; p.23 © Matthew
Ashton/EMPICS; p.27 © Paul Ellis/AP/EMPICS

Every effort has been made to trace all copyright holders, but if any have been
inadvertently overlooked the Publishers will be pleased to make the necessary
arrangements at the first opportunity.

Orders: please contact Bookpoint Ltd, 130 Milton Park, Abingdon, Oxon OX14 4SB.
Telephone: (44) 01235 827720. Fax: (44) 01235 400454. Lines are open 9.00–6.00, Monday
to Saturday, with a 24-hour message answering service. Visit our website at
www.hoddereducation.co.uk

© Mike Wilson 2006
First published in 2006 by
Hodder Murray, an imprint of Hodder Education,
a member of the Hodder Headline Group
338 Euston Road
London NW1 3BH

Impression number   10 9 8 7 6 5 4 3 2 1
Year   2010 2009 2008 2007 2006

Cover photo © Clive Rose/Getty Images
Typeset in 14pt Palatino by SX Composing DTP, Rayleigh, Essex.
Printed in Great Britain by CPI, Bath

A catalogue record for this title is available from the British Library

ISBN-10: 0 340 91413 0
ISBN-13: 978 0340 014 137

Contents

Steven Gerrard: born and bred in Liverpool.

1 Introduction

'I come from a Red house,' says Steven Gerrard.
'All my family are mad about Liverpool.'

Steven has a cousin, Anthony Gerrard.
He plays in blue – for the local rivals Everton.

But Steven has been a Liverpool fan all his life.
To play for Liverpool was his dream come true.

So, how come, in 2005, Steven wanted to leave?
How come he nearly went to Chelsea?

How come he then changed his mind
and stayed at Liverpool?

2 Local Boy

Steven Gerrard was born on 30 May 1980.

He grew up in Whiston.
Whiston is a poor estate near Liverpool.

Steven's dad still goes to all his home games.

He still tells Steven when he has played well.
He also tells him when he plays badly!

Steven's dad took him to his first match,
when Steven was just six.

Steven was spotted by a talent scout
at the age of eight.

'You could just tell,' the scout said.
'He just stood out.
He was the best on the field.'

Steven joined the Liverpool Academy.
At that time, he was small for his age.

At 16 he was still smaller than Michael Owen!
He had some growing to do!

He grew five centimetres in a year.
Now he's 6 feet (184 centimetres) tall,
and he weighs 12 stone (76 kilograms).

3 First Big Match

everton

Steven's first big game
for Liverpool was in 1999.
Steven was 19.
It was against local rivals, Everton.
Liverpool had not won the local derby
for five years.

Steven cleared two shots
off the line.
He helped Liverpool to win 3–2.

'People didn't shut up about it for days!' he said.

It wasn't always that easy.
In his next local derby, Everton won 1–0.
Steven was sent off for two bad tackles!

People didn't shut up about that either!

4 The Player

There is no weak part to Steven's game.

He is strong and very fit.
He can run and run.

He can play left back, or right back.
But he's at his best in midfield.

He can do amazing long passes.
He can do amazing tackles
and come away with the ball.

He can score goals with amazing shots
from outside the box.
He can score with free kicks
from 30 metres.
He can score with his head.

Steven is a born leader.
He was only 23 when he became Liverpool captain.

He can read the game.
He seems to know where the ball is going next.
He can lift his team, and turn games around.

'I play in midfield,' he says,
'but I like to attack as well.

'I like playing in the middle,
but I don't mind playing on the right.

'I like to play for England.
David Beckham and me – we play well together.
We see the game the same way.'

Chelsea manager José Mourinho
wanted to buy Steven.

'He is one of the best in the world,'
Mourinho said.

'He can defend. Then he can attack.

'He has the legs and the power
and the skills to do that.'

Gerrard and Beckham: key England players.

5 England

Steven played his first game
in an England shirt in 2000.
It was his birthday the day before.
He was 20 years old.

After that he was always in the team.

One big highlight of his England career
was beating Germany 5–1 in 2001.
Steven scored one of the goals!

He missed the World Cup in 2002.
He had an injury.

Sven-Göran Eriksson said:
'We will miss Steven.
He is one of the best players
you can find in the world today.'

6 2001 and the Four Trophies!

2001 was a good year for Steven and for Liverpool.

They beat Birmingham in the League Cup Final.
(It was 5–4 after penalties.)

Then they beat Arsenal 2–1 in the FA Cup Final.

In the UEFA Cup Final,
they beat the Spanish side Alavés.
Liverpool got the winning goal
in extra time, and won 5–4.

Liverpool then played Bayern Munich.
(Bayern had won the Champions League.)
Liverpool beat Bayern 3–2
to win the European Super Cup.
Four trophies in one year!

Showing off the silverware!

7 Not All Good News

'I have set myself very high standards,'
Stephen has said.
'But no-one can keep going up and up.'

In 2002, Steven went through a bad spell.

He had back problems.
Some people said he had grown too much, too fast.
His body couldn't take it.

It took time for Steven
to get back to 100 per cent fitness.

His manager said:
'He's having a bad time.
This is not the Steven Gerrard we like!

'We hope he'll come back even stronger.'

Sometimes, Steven has felt
the rest of the team don't keep up
with his high standards.

One time, after a 0–0 draw,
Steven lost his temper with the rest of the team.

'We didn't have a shot on goal
all afternoon!' he said.
'Where is the drive?
Where is the hunger?'

'We are mid-table,' he went on.
'And that's just not good enough.'

Steven began to think that Liverpool
did not seem to share his drive,
his ambition.

At times, Liverpool did not look
like winning anything.
Maybe Steven should think of a move
to another club...

8 Own Goal

When Steven plays well, Liverpool play well.
When Steven plays badly, so do Liverpool.

In February 2005, Liverpool played Chelsea.
It was the Carling Cup Final –
a game Steven would love to forget!

In the first half, Steven missed an open goal.
In the second half, he did score –
but it was for Chelsea!

Devastated.

Chelsea had a free kick.
The ball whipped across the face of the goal,
and Steven headed it into his own net!

Chelsea went on to win 3–2.

Steven felt sick about it.

It felt like his own goal
lost the game for Liverpool.

Steven said:
'To lose any game is painful.
To lose a Cup Final – and score an own goal –
made it a very bad day for me!'

9 Leaving Liverpool?

Steven has always loved Liverpool Football Club.

He loves being at a top club.
He says the managers and trainers know
what they are talking about.

'They have been there.
They have won all the Cups we are now playing in.
When they tell you something
you've got to listen.'

Then, in 2004, Steven began to think again.
He had been with Liverpool for 17 years.
Was it time to move on?

In 17 years, Liverpool had won lots of games.
But they had not won the Premiership.
They were not as good
as the great Liverpool sides of the 1970s.

Steven began to wonder –
did the other players share his dreams?
His ambitions?

His best football was still to come.

Should he stay loyal to Liverpool?
Should he move on
and get the glory with another club?

Steven said:
'I can't wait three or four years
for the club to turn things around.'

In 2004, Chelsea said they wanted to buy Steven.
Steven said no.

Liverpool breathed a sigh of relief.

10 Underdogs

It was May 2005.
Liverpool were in the final
of the Champions League.

There was only one problem.
They were playing AC Milan.
Liverpool were the underdogs.

After one minute, Milan went one up!
Then Milan got another goal.
Offside. A let off for Liverpool.

Then another goal for Milan,
then another.

By half-time, Liverpool were 3–0 down!
There was no way back
against a team like AC Milan.

'At half-time,' Steven said,
'I had my head in my hands.

'I knew it was all over.
I didn't think at any point we were going to win.'

Five minutes into the second half,
Steven headed a goal.
Liverpool began to believe.

A minute later, they got another goal.
3–2 – only one goal behind!

Ten minutes later, Steven won a penalty.
He was pushed over in the penalty box.
Liverpool scored and it was 3–3!

'By that time,' Steven said,
'We were running on empty.
We really needed the game to go to penalties.'

Milan missed their first penalty
– and their second!

Steven said:
'That's when I knew it was going to be our day!'

Liverpool had been the underdogs.
They had been 3–0 down.
Yet they had come back.
They won the penalty shoot-out 3–2.

All the Liverpool players
went up and got their medals.
Then Steven, the captain,
picked up the Champions League Cup.
The fans went wild!

That night, Steven went to sleep
with the Cup in his bed.
'I didn't want to let go of it!' he said.

'The Cup is heavy, but it feels good!'

Ecstatic: Gerrard holds the Champions League cup aloft.

11   How Could I Leave?

'How could I leave Liverpool,' Steven asked,
'after a night like that?
It was the best night of my life!'

Steven was a world-class player.
He'd showed that.
He'd showed he could fight – and win.

That's why Chelsea offered to buy him again.
They offered £32 million –
a new UK record.

Liverpool said:
'For Steven, it's not about money.
It's about success.
We want Steven
to stay here all his life.'

They gave Steven a pay rise –
an extra £1 million a year.

There was talk of building the team.
There was talk that Michael Owen might come back.
There was talk that Luis Figo
might come to Liverpool.

Steven was still in two minds.
Then some fans got hold of a Liverpool shirt.
It was Steven's famous number 8 shirt –
with his name on the back.
They set fire to it.

That's what really made up his mind.
That's when Steven knew what he means to the fans.

He didn't want to be called a traitor.
Liverpool FC meant too much to him.

'I never said I wanted to leave,'
Steven said later.
'But I thought the club didn't want me.
I felt I was being backed into a corner.
If I blame anyone, I blame myself.

Steven couldn't leave these adoring fans behind.

'Now I'm just happy it's all sorted.
I'm doing what I wanted to do all along –
to stay at Liverpool.'

Is that the end of the story?
Or just the end of a chapter?

Every big club wants to sign Steven Gerrard.
Maybe they will try again.

He is young.
He's world-class.
And his best days are still to come.